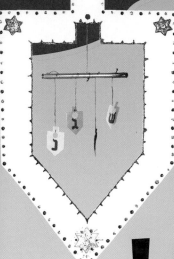

Fun Holiday Crafts
Kids Can Do!

Hanukkah Crafts

Karen E. Bledsoe

E| Enslow Publishers, Inc.

40 Industrial Road   PO Box 38
Box 398   Aldershot
Berkeley Heights, NJ 07922 Hants GU12 6BP
USA   UK

http://www.enslow.com

Library of Congress Cataloging-in-Publication Data

Bledsoe, Karen E.
    Hanukkah crafts / Karen E. Bledsoe.
        p. cm. — (Fun holiday crafts kids can do)
    Summary: Provides information about the origin and customs of Hanukkah, ideas for celebrating this holiday, and directions for making such crafts as a dreidel mobile, holiday cards, and candle candy holders.
    Includes bibliographical references and index.
    ISBN 0-7660-2238-2
    1. Jewish crafts—Juvenile literature. 2. Hanukkah—Juvenile literature. [1. Jewish crafts. 2. Hanukkah. 3. Handicraft.] I. Title. II. Series.
BM729.H35B55 2004
296.4'35—dc22
                                        2003012074

Printed in the United States of America

10 9 8 7 6 5 4 3 2 1

To Our Readers: We have done our best to make sure all Internet addresses in this book were active and appropriate when we went to press. However, the author and the publisher have no control over and assume no liability for the material available on those Internet sites or on other Web sites they may link to. Any comments or suggestions can be sent by e-mail to comments@enslow.com or to the address on the back cover.

Illustration Credits: Crafts prepared by June Ponte.
                            Photography by Carl Feryok.

Cover Illustration: Carl Feryok

Contents

Safety Note: Be sure to ask for help from an adult, if
needed, to complete these crafts!

introduction

Hanukkah is also called the Festival of Lights. This holiday celebrates a great miracle that Jewish people believe happened more than two thousand years ago.

King Antiochus ruled the kingdom of Judea. He wanted Jewish people in Judea to worship Greek gods, as he did. They refused. So he ordered his soldiers to destroy the temple, the Jews' place of worship in Jerusalem. The soldiers ruined the temple. They

took the holy lamp, called the menorah, which had always been kept burning with special oil. For the first time, the menorah flames went out.

Brave Jewish fighters fought the soldiers in many battles. Led by Judah Maccabee, the Jews won. They fixed the temple and replaced the menorah. But even though they had only enough oil to last for one day, the menorah flames burned for eight days!

Hanukkah celebrates the Jews' victory over the king's soldiers. The holiday lasts for eight days. Each night, menorah candles are lit. Presents are given. Children play a game with a dreidel, a small top. On the dreidel's four sides are Hebrew letters. They stand for the words *Nes Gadol Hayah Sham*, which means "A great miracle happened there!"

Dreidel Mobile

Celebrate the Hanukkah season with this fun mobile.

What You Will Need:

- pencil
- thin cardboard
- scissors
- paint, markers, or glitter glue
- hole punch
- thread or thin string
- drinking straw
- colored paper

1. Use a pencil to trace a large dreidel shape onto thin cardboard. Use the pattern on page 26, if you like. Cut a large dreidel shape out of cardboard.

2. Cut a smaller dreidel shape from the center of the large dreidel, leaving a frame about 1 inch wide all around. This large dreidel outline will be the frame for your mobile. Decorate the frame on both sides with paint, markers, or glitter glue.

3. Punch a hole at the top of the frame. Tie a piece of thread or thin string through the hole for hanging your mobile when it is done.

4. Punch another hole just above the cut-out area on the inside of the frame. Tie the straw to it with thread or thin string so that the straw hangs like a bar near the top of the cut-out area. Cut the straw to fit within the frame.

5. Cut four small dreidel shapes from colored paper. Draw one of the four Hebrew letters (see page 26) on both sides of each small dreidel.

6. Punch a hole in the top of each shape. Hang the shapes from the straw with thread or thin string. Now hang your mobile where a breeze will catch it, and enjoy!

Carefully cut out the
large dreidel frame . . .

Decorate it with
lots of color . . .

Carefully cut out the
smaller dreidels . . .

Your mobile is
ready for display!

Holiday Hint:

Instead of Hebrew letters, you
may choose to paste pictures of
friends, family, or drawings of
favorite Hanukkah activities
on the dreidels.

Helping Hands Menorah

This menorah is fun to make.

What You Will Need:

- blue and white felt squares
- white glue
- square cardboard

- envelope
- pencil
- scrap paper
- scissors

- marker
- yellow or orange felt
- glitter glue or glitter glaze

1. Glue the blue felt to the cardboard. Let it dry. Then, glue the envelope to the back of the cardboard with the flap out.

2. To make a pattern for your menorah, draw a candlestick shape in the center of the scrap paper. Make four more candles to the left of it by tracing around the four fingers of your left hand. Do the same on the right, using your right hand.

3. Use your pattern to cut the menorah shape out of white felt. Glue the white felt "menorah" to the blue felt.

4. Cut nine flame shapes from yellow or orange felt. Decorate them with glitter glue or glitter glaze. Glue one of them to the center candlestick. Put the other eight in the envelope on the back of the cardboard.

5. Starting at the right and working toward the left, add one flame to your menorah for each night of Hanukkah. On the eighth night, your Helping Hands Menorah will be complete!

After gluing the felt to the front of the cardboard, glue an envelope to the back . . .

Carefully cut out the "candles" . . .

Glue the candles onto the blue felt . . .

Make a flame for each of the candles. . .

Your menorah is ready to light up the Hannukah nights!

Holiday Hint:

Take turns with friends or family members, "lighting" one candle each night. As you light the candle, tell the others about a time when they have helped you.

9

Embossed Place Cards

These place cards will shine on your holiday table.

What You Will Need:

- dark colored construction paper
- scissors
- aluminum foil
- white paper
- black marker
- newspaper
- blunt pencil or paintbrush
- white glue

1. Fold the construction paper in half with the short ends together. Cut along the fold. Fold one of the pieces in half again.

2. Cut a piece of aluminum foil and a piece of white paper the same size as the folded construction paper.

3. Write a person's name on the white paper with the marker. Turn the paper over. If you cannot read the name through the paper, go over it again.

4. Lay the foil shiny side down on folded newspaper. Place the paper with the name upside down on the foil.

5. Use a blunt pencil or the pointed end of a paintbrush to trace the name into the foil.

6. Remove the paper. Make the lines deeper on the foil if they are hard to read.

7. Glue the foil shiny side up onto the folded construction paper.

Cut a piece of construction paper in half . . .

Fold it in half . . .

Write a name on the foil . . .

Glue the foil to the construction paper and your place card is done!

Holiday Hint:

A set of place cards would make a very special Hanukkah gift for your family!

Hanukkah Symbol Stamps

Here's a fun way to decorate paper projects.

What You Will Need:

- small blocks of wood
- craft foam
- felt-tipped pen
- scissors
- craft glue
- ink pad

1. Trace the outline of a wooden block on the craft foam using a felt-tipped pen. Cut the shape out.

2. Draw a Hanukkah symbol, such as a dreidel or Star of David, on the cut-out foam. If you like, use the patterns on page 27.

3. Cut out the symbol. Make straight snips with the scissors to turn corners on the foam.

4. Glue the foam shape to the wooden block using craft glue. Let it dry overnight.

5. Press the stamp on the ink pad and stamp away!

Get a block
of wood . . .

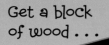

Trace the block
and draw a
symbol on the
foam . . .

Carefully cut the
symbol out and glue
it onto the block . . .

Grab an ink pad and
your stamp is ready
to decorate!

Holiday Hint:

Use different colored ink pads
with your Hanukkah stamps. See
what interesting patterns you
can create.

13

Hanukkah Magnets

These are easy to make and so useful!

What You Will Need:

- pen or pencil
- craft foam
- miniature Hanukkah cookie cutters (optional)
- scissors
- glitter glue or other decorations
- white glue
- small magnets or magnetic strips

1. With a pen or a pencil, draw the shapes you want on craft foam. Make them about 1 or 2 inches long. Miniature Hanukkah cookie cutters make good tracing patterns, but you can also use the patterns on page 27.

2. Cut out the shapes.

3. Decorate the shapes using glitter glue or any other decorations you like. Let the shapes dry.

4. On the back of each shape, glue a magnet or magnetic strip. Let the glue dry.

Carefully cut out
different shapes . . .

Glue a magnet
on the back . . .

Decorate your magnets
with lots of different
colored glitter glue!

Holiday Hint:

Stick Hanukkah reminders
on the refrigerator with
these magnets.

Holiday Cards

Send Hanukkah greetings with a handmade card.

What You Will Need:

- blue construction paper
- white paper
- white glue
- scissors

- construction paper in various colors
- glitter glue, stickers, paint, markers, crayons (optional)
- pen or pencil

1. Fold the blue paper in half so that the shorter ends meet.

2. Fold a piece of white paper in half the same way.

3. Open the blue paper. Put a thin line of glue down one side of the fold. Place the folded edge of the white paper on the glue. It should line up with the blue paper fold. Let it dry.

4. Decorate the front of the card. Glue on some Hanukkah symbols cut from construction paper.

5. If you like, make your card extra special with glitter glue, stickers, paint, markers, or crayons. Let the decorations dry.

6. Write your message inside with a pen or pencil.

Decorate the front
of the card . . .

Glue a piece of white
paper inside . . .

Happy Hanukkah!

Write a special
holiday message!

Happy Hanukkah!

Holiday Hint:

Handmade cards show that you
really care. This is a nice
Hanukkah gift for someone who
is important to you!

Star of David Ornament

This ornament glows with pretty colors.

What You Will Need:

- black marker
- black construction paper
- ruler

- scissors
- colored tissue paper
- glue stick

1. Draw a Star of David on construction paper with the black marker (if you like, use the pattern on page 28). Make it as large possible. Use a ruler to make sure the lines are straight.

2. Draw lines ½ inch inside the lines of the star, as shown.

3. Cut out the star. Then cut out the spaces in the points and in the middle. The side with the marker is the back.

4. Cut a piece of tissue paper a bit larger than one of the openings.

5. Spread glue around the edges of the opening on the side with the marker on it. Glue the tissue paper to the back of each section. If necessary, cut away extra tissue paper.

6. Do the same for all the openings. You can use just blue and white tissue paper, or any bright colors you like.

Carefully cut out a Star of David . . .

Glue colored tissue paper into the open sections . . .

You can use different colors for each section . . .

Your ornament is ready to be hung in a window!

Holiday Hint:

Tape your Star of David ornament to a window. When light shines through it, the colors will shine like stained glass.

19

Collage Bookmarks

These colorful bookmarks can be used over and over.

What You Will Need:

- pencil
- ruler
- blue construction paper
- scissors
- cotton swabs

- white glue
- white and blue tissue paper
- silver tissue or ribbon
- clear self-adhesive vinyl, such as Contac® paper

1. Draw a 2- by 6-inch rectangle on blue construction paper. Cut it out.

2. Cut the tissue paper into ¾-inch squares.

3. Spread glue with a cotton swab on the blue paper rectangle.

4. Glue on white and blue tissue squares to cover the rectangle. They should overlap.

5. Cut silver tissue or ribbon into tiny strips or squares. Glue some onto the tissue paper. Let dry.

6. Cut a 3- by 7-inch piece of clear self-adhesive vinyl.

7. Stick the tissue side of the bookmark to the vinyl. Leave a ½-inch border of vinyl all around.

8. Fold the vinyl over the back of the bookmark. Press down. Your bookmark is done!

Start with a piece of construction paper . . .

Cut out little pieces of tissue paper or ribbon . . .

Put it all together and you'll have a wonderful bookmark to give to a friend or family member!

Holiday Hint:

These collage bookmarks are fun to make and give as gifts. Change the colors of the papers to match the seasons or holidays.

Dreidel Beaded Key Chain

You will always find your keys with this handy key chain.

What You Will Need:

- ruler
- lacing or cord
- scissors
- blue and yellow pony beads
- key ring

1. Cut a 5-foot-long piece of lacing or cord. String one blue bead on the cord. Push it to the middle.

2. Slip the ends of the lacing or cord through three more beads. Pull tight to make the dreidel point (see photos on page 23).

3. Put four blue beads on one end of the cord. Slip the other end through the beads from the other side. Pull tight.

4. Make the next row the same way, using five beads. Use six beads for the row after that.

5. Use seven beads on each of the next four rows. If you make a mistake, pull the cord out of the beads and try again.

6. For the next row, put two beads on one end of the cord and five on the other. Take the end that has two beads and put it through the first three beads on the other cord. Pull tight.

7. Make two more rows with three beads each for the dreidel stem.

8. Tie the ends of the cord in a knot. Then, tie the ends around the key ring.

Start with
one bead . . .

Follow the steps to string
on more beads . . .

Keep adding
more beads . . .

Add a key ring and
you are all done!

Holiday Hint:

This key chain makes a great
Hanukkah gift for a friend.

Candle Candy Holders

These candy holders are easy to make and use.

What You Will Need:

- toilet paper tubes
- colored paper
- clear tape
- markers
- glitter glue
- yellow cellophane or tissue paper
- ruler
- pencil
- scissors
- candy or tiny gifts

1. Cover a toilet paper tube with colored paper. Tape the paper into place.

2. Decorate the paper tube with markers, glitter glue, or anything you like.

3. Cut a 12-inch (or larger) square of cellophane or tissue paper.

4. Make a pocket in the middle of the cellophane or tissue paper. Fill the pocket with candy or tiny gifts.

5. Twist the cellophane or tissue paper over the top of the treats. Wrap tape around the twist.

6. Tape the treat bundle inside the tube. Stick the corners of the cellophane out over the top of the tube to look like a flame.

7. If you like, add a few dots of glitter glue for sparkle.

Decorate a toilet paper tube . . .

Place candy in some tissue paper . . .

Tape it closed. . .

Tape the tissue paper candy packet in the tube and your gift is ready!

Holiday Hint:

Make these candle candy holders as party favors. Fill them with gelt, or gold-wrapped chocolate coins, for a sweet Hanukkah treat.

25

Patterns

Use tracing paper to copy the patterns on these pages. Ask an adult to help you cut and trace the shapes onto construction paper.

Enlarge by 150%

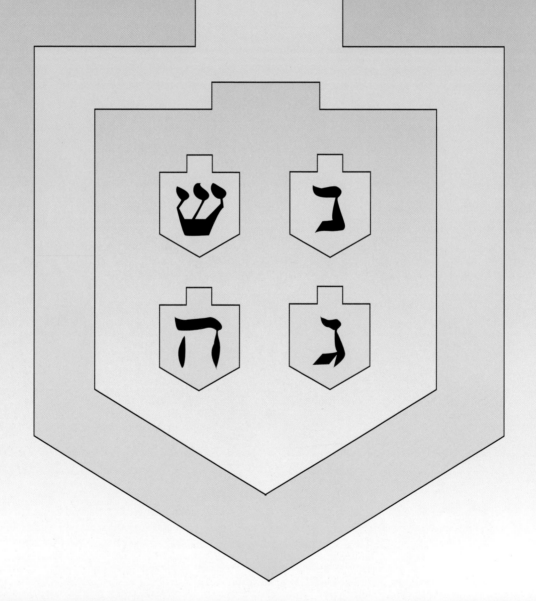

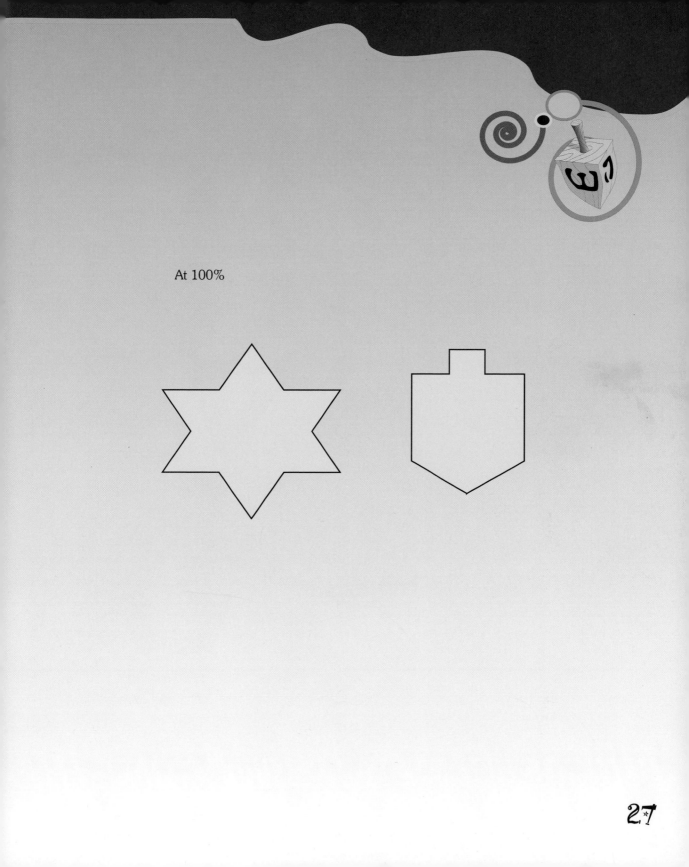

At 100%

Enlarge by 122%

Words to Know

dreidel—A small top used in a game during Hanukkah. There are Hebrew letters on the sides of the dreidel. The letters tell the players what to do in the game.

gelt—Money or chocolate coins, which children receive as gifts during Hanukkah.

Hanukkah—The Jewish Festival of Lights. This holiday celebrates a Jewish victory over Greek soldiers long ago.

menorah—A special candleholder that holds nine candles. The center candle is used to light one additional candle each night of Hanukkah.

Star of David—A six-pointed star that is a symbol of the Jewish faith.

Reading About Hanukkah

Agranoff, Tracey. *Kids Love Jewish Holiday Crafts.* New York: Pitspopany Press, 2000.

Marx, David F. *Chanukah.* New York: Children's Press, 2000.

O'Hare, Jeff. *Hanukkah, Festival of Lights: Celebrate With Songs, Decorations, Food, Games, Prayers, and Traditions.* Honesdale, Pa.: Boyds Mills Press, 2000.

Rosinsky, Natalie M. *Hanukkah.* Minneapolis: Compass Point Books, 2002.

Ross, Kathy and Melinda Levine. *The Jewish Holiday Craft Book.* Brookfield, Conn.: Millbrook Press, 1997.

Schaefer, Lola M. *Hanukkah.* Mankato, Minn.: Pebble Books, 2001.

Internet Addresses

Akhlah—The Jewish Children's Learning Network
<http://www.akhlah.com>

Thebestkidsbooksite.com—Creative Hanukkah Crafts
<http://www.thebestkidsbooksite.com/
hanukkahcrafts.cfm>

Index